ALA MOTORCYCLE

Are you sure you know what you are doing?

By Airborne Andy

ISBN-13: 978-1482367317
ISBN-10: 1482367319

TABLE OF CONTENTS

Ah... but where to begin. In this case, perhaps the end is a good place to start. I'm selling my trusty motorcycle.

For Sale:

Slightly used Suzuki DR650. Only ridden off-road a few times in Mexico, across the U.S. and Bolivia. Only taken on a few road trips from Los Angeles to Maine, Florida, Alaska and Argentina. Only exposed to salt water during a sailboat trip from Panama to Colombia, and for a short ride across the flooded Salar de Uyuni. Only raced once - in the Baja 1000. And, only been down 25 maybe 30 times. New air in tires.

For many years I had dreamed of riding a motorcycle across the country but the farthest I had managed was from California to Oregon (the next state over). I had also often thought about taking a trip into the Alaskan wilderness. I'd been quite active and adventurous for most of my life but my physical abilities had begun to decline noticeably. For the past year I had suffered from Plantar Fasciitis – a painful aliment in the arches of the feet – and at times I could barely walk. With the realization that I was growing old much faster than I had anticipated, I decided it was time for one last adventure – one last hurrah before fading into sunset of my life. But what could I do... what adventure could I undertake with my waning physical abilities? It appeared that I already had the answer - Alaska by motorcycle would be my last great adventure!

I searched the internet for information on riding a motorcycle to Alaska. That's how I discovered the Adventure Rider web-site (advrider.com). There I found lots of helpful information, stories and photos from others that had already ridden to Alaska. I scoured the web-site reading lots of reports. I discovered that there was an annual motorcycle gathering - the Dust to Dawson Run - which takes place in Dawson City, in the Yukon Territories of Canada, during summer solstice. And, I learned that there were three infamous dirt highways that attracted adventurous riders from all over the globe – the Dempster, the Denali, and the Dalton highways – which became the highlights of my travel plan.

I had ridden motorcycles on and off since I was a child and had just recently gotten back into riding. But, I didn't have the right type of motorcycle for this particular journey. At the time, I owned and rode a Triumph Bonneville – a street bike with classic styling. The trip to Alaska would include lots of miles on the famed "Alcan Highway" which crossed the vast and unforgivingly remote regions of Canada and Alaska, and was often under (re)construction in numerous areas due to constant deterioration from the severe climate conditions. These "Construction Zones" were unpaved and often rough dirt for many miles. I also wanted to experience the notorious 3Ds – the Dempster, the Denali, and the Dalton highways – with a combined, round-trip distance of nearly 2,000 miles of dirt and gravel. So although my journey included many thousands of miles of paved roads, the thorough enjoyment of this epic adventure would require a motorcycle with some dirt in its pedigree. I figured that the ideal motorcycle for this type of adventure would be a Dual-Sport. Dual-Sports are small to medium size bikes that are designed for both on-road and off-road use. There are also some larger "Adventure" bikes that would be enjoyable in this type of terrain but generally speaking - larger bikes are more road-biased and smaller bikes are more dirt-biased. Considering all of the above, I chose a medium sized bike with a simple low tech design, renowned for its capable manors both on and off road, and for its legendary reliability akin to that of a claw hammer - the venerable Suzuki DR650.

I had been planning my Alaska trip for a few weeks. I hadn't even begun my journey yet and already I felt like a world traveler. The day before I was scheduled to leave, I packed everything on the bike and took it for a test ride just to make sure everything worked alright. Down the road a short distance, I stopped at a local convenience store for some coffee and started talking to the guy behind the counter. He saw all my gear on the bike and asked me where I was going. When I told him I was going to Alaska he really got interested. It turned out that he was an avid motorcycle enthusiast too. He told me he was from Sri Lanka and loved to ride. He said the bikes there were limited to 250cc but the police rode 400's. Then he asked me if I was moving, which sounded odd to me at the time but looking back at the haphazard looking way in which my bike was packed, I could see why he might think that – it looked like something out of an old Beverly Hillbillies television show.

A short while later I pulled up to a stoplight next to a friend and his wife in their car. They honked and waived. Later my friend confessed that he didn't recognize me at first and remarked to his wife: "Look at that poor bastard with everything he owns packed up on the back of that motorcycle!"

Packed and ready for my first long-distance motorcycle adventure

I left Los Angeles, the following day with a month of vacation and no real plan other than heading north. Although, I did hope to make it to Dawson City in the Yukon for the annual "Dust to Dawson" run. And, I wanted to ride the three infamous dirt highways: the Dempster, the Denali, and the Dalton.

What follows is a daily journal of my trip – I hope you enjoy it.

(Miles: 360)

I couldn't decide if I wanted to take the slower, scenic and fun twisty route up the coast, or go for the Interstate Highway and make better time. I opted for the twisties and headed up California's coast on the famous Pacific Coast Highway. I had ridden highway 1 (PCH) several times before so I knew that it would be a treat. The view was beautiful and my state of mind was serene - I was finally on my way.

Before leaving, I had thought about getting some hard shell side-bags to carry some of my gear but decided against them as I'd read that they can cause injury in a crash – and they were fairly expensive. I had also struggled finding just the right windscreen to put on my bike for the long trip and ended up with one that was rather tall. It was great for blocking the wind but kept getting blown back in my face. I finally got it setup so that it would stay in place and made my way up the extremely beautiful coastline to Big Sur where I camped the first night.

I was a little worried that I didn't have enough warm clothing as I was wearing all my cold weather gear to keep warm while riding and I hadn't even left California yet - what would I do when it really got cold?

The scenic Pacific Coast Highway

(Miles: 500, crashes: 1)

Excited to be starting my big adventure, I decided to have my cake and eat it too - I wanted to take the fun scenic, twisty route but still make good time. So I got up early the next morning and left Big Sur heading north on the legendary Pacific Coast Highway. After a couple hours in the curves I was getting pretty fast and forgot that I had 50 pounds of gear on the back seat – Ooops! I leaned over a little too far going around a slow 20 mph switchback and the front wheel washed out - down I went, sliding across the pavement and into a ditch!

Luckily, someone upstairs must like me. A guy stopped to help me pick up the bike and it started after only a couple stabs at the starter. I looked the bike over and discovered that nothing was broken - NOTHING! And, nothing seemed to be broken on ME either! My elbow hurt a little so I removed my jacket and had a look, just to be sure. Wow, it was a bit swollen but I wasn't bleeding and everything seemed to be working. My goofy highway foot pegs, which I fabricated at the last minute, kept the bike from hitting anything in front and the big rack I had installed kept the back of the bike safe. The only damage was some minor scratches on the left mirror, front fender, rack, and wind screen.

Awesome! IM ALIVE!!! ...and I'm going to Alaska!

My disheveled bike and gear after the crash

Within a few days my outer forearm turned completely black
from my elbow to my wrist

Other than the crash, the ride was fantastic and the view was too. And, I was being a bit more careful. But, suddenly the engine started to cut out so I figured I was getting low on fuel and reached down to flip the gas switch over to reserve - it didn't help. So I pulled off the road and after checking a few things, figured out that my backpack, which I had strapped to the gas tank, was pinching the air breather tube. Ah... an easy fix and I was on my way again. A few hundred miles later, and guess what? The motor died. No problem, this time I figured it probably was getting low on fuel. So, I reached down to flip the gas switch over to reserve... and, guess what? It was already on reserve! I had forgot to flip it back to the "ON" position earlier when I "THOUGHT" I was getting low on fuel but really wasn't. And now, I was in the middle of nowhere in northern California - Humbolt County, land of the Wildwood Weed... nothing but trees. No problem! I had AAA Roadside Assistance. One quick call and they would bring me some gas. OK... did I have a cell-phone signal? YES, I did! But, when I called AAA, before I could tell them where I was, my cell-phone battery died. *Hmmm... I must have used up all my good luck back in the crash.* So, I flagged someone down, and borrowed their cell-phone. An hour later, I had gas and was on my way again.

(Miles: 300)

Not too much excitement on my 3rd day – Thank God. My hands were a bit stiff and a little sore. I wasn't use to such long days on a thumper (a single cylinder motorcycle). But I think the many hundreds of miles of twisty roads may have contributed as well.

It was a short mileage day and I cut over from the scenic coastal road to the super-slab Interstate 5 Freeway, trading a beautiful view for expedient passage. There is a short weather window for riding a motorcycle into Northern Canada and Alaska. The ideal time frame is from June to September but it could possibly stretch a month on either side depending on the weather that year.

I stopped, in Salem Oregon and visited with family before continuing on my journey. I only had a month for my trip so it was just a short stopover and I was on the road again.

Day 4 - Salem, Oregon, USA to Whistler, British Columbia, Canada

(Miles: 407)

It felt good to be on the road and I was anxious to get out into the vast wilderness of the north. But I was a little concerned about going into the remote regions of Canada and Alaska without some sort of personal protection for self-defense against bears. I made the mistake of searching the internet for videos of Bear Attacks and learned that they are not only large and powerful but they are also fast and surprisingly agile. One rather dramatic video showed a Grizzly Bear fighting a large Elk in a shallow river – the Elk tried to fend off the Bear with its horns and was successful for a while. But the surprisingly athletic bear eventually got ahold of the Elk's horns and wrestled him down, drowning him in the river. I also learned that bears will usually avoid humans if they hear them coming – that's why some hikers wear bells when travelling thru bear country. However, in some national parks bears have been known to track hikers wearing bells.

Call me crazy - but I like to know that I can defend myself in ANY situation! So I thought about picking up a short pump shotgun. I knew that a shotgun was poor choice for hunting Bears but I only wanted it for defense – and I figured that a few shots to the face at point blank range would seriously dissuade any creature on earth. However, I discovered that no one in Oregon or Washington would sell me a gun because I was from California. How Bizarre was that? So, I bought a bowie knife instead. Not as powerful as a shotgun, but better than nothing. And, I decided to buy some Bear Spray (basically an oversize, industrial strength, pepper spray cartridge) once I crossed the border into Canada - you cannot bring Bear Spray across the border - guns yes, Bear Spray no.

I also bought a fishing rod. And, while I was in the parking lot at the Sporting Goods store packing my new knife and fishing rod away on the bike a woman started talking to me about my trip. And, she told me her sister had a cabin in Fairbanks and gave me her number. *"Hmmm... people seem much friendlier to strangers here than back in Los Angeles"* I thought.

Then I headed for the Canadian border. When I arrived, I was interrogated by immigrations about where I was going... what I was going to do... how much money I had... How long I was staying... It all seemed kind of strange to me at the time. But when I inquired, they said that they just wanted to be sure I didn't become stranded in Canada. Once again looking back at the appearance of my expertly packed adventure bike, I could understand their concerns. They also asked if I had any guns and didn't even flinch when I said that I had a Bowie knife. After a while they decide that I was harmless and wouldn't become a burden on the Canadian taxpayers, and they let me go thru.

I spent the next hour trying to find my way out of Vancouver, British Columbia - I was totally lost and getting frustrated. When I finally got out of the city going the right direction up the 99, I got my first taste of the incredible scenery in the southwestern part of Canada. I also, got my first taste of the Construction Zones and it ended up taking much longer than I thought. Fortunately, the view along the 99 was extraordinarily beautiful. I finally set up camp just below Whistler - another long day with short mileage but it was well worth the wait.

(Miles: 481)

I got an early start and headed up over the Lillooet range – all I can say is that the 99 is one fantastic road. In fact it was more fun than any road I had ever ridden. And it was tailor made for a Dual-Sport motorcycle. Although it was all paved, much of it was in rather poor condition which actually made it more fun, dodging the holes, jumping cracks, and picking good lines through the flawed pavement. As I started up one pass, there was a sign that said: Warning Extreme Grades! And they weren't kidding – it was an incredibly steep, winding path thru the mountains, zigzagging up and down back and forth, sometimes smooth, sometimes rough - fantastic fun! And the scenery was just as amazing. I would have taken more pictures but I was having too much fun riding.

Along the 99 in the Lillooet Range

After heading down the other side of the pass, the weather started moving in. You could see big patches of puffy rain clouds all over with small traces of blue sky in between. But, lady luck was with me and I always seemed to be going between the clouds. Too bad it wouldn't last.

(Miles: 534)

Excited to continue my journey, I got another early start and my first glimpse of wildlife. I was just cruising along, around a bend, and there it was... this enormous moose with its baby walking along the side of the road. I was a little startled and slowed down because I didn't really know what they were going to do. Then they just turned and trotted away. For some reason it just seemed to throw me way off. After that, I noticed that I had slowed down by about 10 mph and couldn't seem to get back on pace. Maybe I was thinking there might be another surprise around the next bend.

A while later I started thinking that I must have missed my gas stop - although I wasn't sure how. Before my trip I had ordered and received a copy of Alaska's travel Bible: The Milepost (www.milepost.com) – it's a guide to the roads, ferries, lodging and services along the routes throughout western Canada and Alaska. The wild and uninhabited nature of the enormous, remote areas should not to be taken lightly. You certainly don't want to run out of gas there, especially on a motorcycle! And, sometimes it is a fairly long distance between fuel stops. So, I started trying to calculate, in my head, if I had enough fuel to make it to the next gas. I thought it would be close but I could probably make it if I rode slowly enough and conserved fuel. And, I decided that 40 mph would give me a good shot at making it. So there I was, motoring along at a leisurely pace thru a very beautiful but desolate stretch of woods, kicking myself for possibly missing a fuel stop. Then I came up over a small rise and guess what I saw standing in front of me, right in the middle of the road... A F%$&%ing BEAR! ...standing right on the white line! I immediately started going thru my options, in my head... should I go left, should I go right, should I gun it, or stop and try to turn around? But before I could do anything, he just turned and trotted away. My heart was beating pretty fast and I was thinking, "MAN THAT WAS CLOSE!" But I was quite literally "not out of the woods yet!" And, I could still run out of gas! What if there was another bear in those woods? There was a pretty good chance of that!

Might I even have to defend myself against a bear, with a bowie knife? Yikes! Next stop... a sporting goods store for some Bear Strength, Pepper Spray! Then I would at least have a chance... pepper spray AND a bowie knife! DOH!

Anyway, I made it to the gas station. And, I stopped at a sporting goods store in Dawson Creek and picked up a can of Bear Spray. BUT.... later that day... I ...Uh... well...... I...... I.... RAN OUT OF GAS! There! I said it! *Unbelievable! How could I do that! I can't believe it!* Fortunately, I ran out of gas right next to a camp ground. So, I pushed my bike to the entrance and proceeded to beat myself up... verbally abuse and belittle myself. *What an Idiot! How could I run out of gas again! I'm not telling anyone about this!* Then I saw an animal on the side of the road, some distance away. It looked like a dog, maybe a coyote or a fox. *Hmmm... where's that Bear Spray? Perhaps I should test fire it just to familiarize myself with my new weapon of choice.* So I got out the Bear Spray, removed the safety clip, and fired it down wind - just one quick burst - It shot like a fire extinguisher with a range of about 15 feet. *OK, cool.* So I put it away and headed down into the camp grounds, in search of people. I found a few folks in motor homes and managed to get about a liter of gas - enough to travel about 12 miles. The guy that gave me the gas said he thought there was a station up the road about 5 miles. *Great!* So, off I went. But, when I got to the gas station, it was closed. It should have been open – it was only about 5:00 pm. I looked around – it was a small settlement with just a few buildings. There was a work camp right next to the gas station but it appeared to be abandoned. There's was also a Bed & Breakfast across the street so I tried there with no luck – they had no fuel to spare. Then I rode back to a farm house that I saw on my way in from the campground. No one was there, except for a few dogs that gladly chased me. There was nothing else around. So I went back to the gas station and parked in front of the pump. *What now?* It had been about 3 hours since I ran out of gas and it looked like it may be quite a few more before I could get any. It was 50 miles to the next station so I was stuck right there. Now, I'm not a religious man. But, I am a spiritual person - even if somewhat reluctantly. And, I do believe in some sort of higher power. And, now seemed like it might be a good time to... oh... I don't know... maybe pray - maybe just one quick little prayer. What the heck!

"God, please send someone to bring me some gas!"

No sooner had this last thought occurred, than I hear: Bbbbbbbbbb...Bbbbbbbbbb... Bbbbbbbbbbbbbbbbbb....

I look up ... almost in shock ... as a young boy and girl on a quad come riding up. "Do you need gas?" Now I'm holding back tears! Yes, I do. The boy say's that someone ran into the gas pump yesterday and that's why the station is closed. But, he thinks he knows someone he can get some gas from and he rides off. Ten minutes later, he comes back empty handed but says he will try someone else. Twenty minutes later, he returns with about two gallons of gas - more than enough to get me to the next station. Oh My God!

The sign at the start of the Alcan Highway in Dawson Creek

The Kiskatinaw Bridge at mile 21 along the "Old" Alcan Highway

Day 7 - Summit Lake, British Columbia to Whitehorse, Yukon

(Miles: 474)

It had been raining all around me for the past few days. But to that point I had somehow been able to avoid getting wet, although sometimes by the narrowest of margins – kind of like a storm chaser in reverse: Airborne Andy - Storm Dodger! Anyway, my luck finally ran out. It started raining during the night and was still raining when I woke up. So, I sat there in my tent writing a list of all the fuel stops along my route so I would be sure not to run out of gas again.

I had been staying in established campgrounds since I started my trip. There were certainly opportunities to camp out for free in the remote wilderness areas I was travelling through but I felt a little more secure camping in established sites where other people were usually nearby.

After putting on my rain gear, I broke camp and descended to lower ground where the weather was clear. I would stop periodically as photo opportunities arose. During one such Kodak moment, I pulled off of the road and down to the river bank to get a picture. Then when I went to leave, I tipped the bike over. To make matters worse, with the weight of all my gear stacked up high on the back rack, I couldn't pick it up. I had to unload all my gear from the bike so I could stand it back up. And of course I lost some gas while my bike was lying on its side so it was going to be close making it to the next fuel station... AGAIN!

Now if you ask me, there's a litmus test for every great adventure... it's that "moment of clarity" that comes from pushing beyond perceived limitations and experiencing repeated hardships or failures. I believe that this moment of clarity occurs at least once during every great adventure. And out of that brief epiphany arises a single question:

What the "#%@*" am I doing here?

At that point my journey had not yet crossed over into what I would consider a great adventure but it was moving in that direction. It was a long, wet day so and I got use to riding in the rain but I did make it to the next gas station. However, I had a long journey ahead of me and plenty of time to second guess my decision to go there in the first place. Would it be a Great Adventure? Only time would tell.

My bike just before it tipped over

Muncho Lake on the Alcan in Northern BC

Near the Sign Post Forest in Watson Lake I met up with 3 other riders (Lydia, Bob and Dan). The Sign Post Forest is a huge collection of signs that people brought from all over - it is a very famous landmark on the Alcan Highway. After talking for a bit we all rode together for the next few hours before stopping in Whitehorse for the night.

The Sign Post Forest at Watson Lake in the Yukon Territories

Bob, Dan, and Lidia getting directions to a restaurant in
Whitehorse

(Miles: 0)

I decided to stay in Whitehorse for another day and do some maintenance on my bike. Lidia, who was from Vancouver British Columbia, was heading to Alaska and decided to go south to Skagway and catch the ferry back to Vancouver. She was riding a Triumph Bonneville just like the one I had back home. Bob and Dan were from Montreal, Quebec in eastern Canada and were also headed for Alaska. They got a camp site at the RV Park and I decide to do the same.

After setting up camp, I changed my oil and rearranged my gear to put the center of gravity lower with some homemade soft side-bags (two soft coolers tied together) – I couldn't find any real soft side-bags in town so I improvised. They would work for the time being and at least the bike handled better than it did with everything stacked up high on the rear rack. I put all my heavy stuff like tools in the side-bags which placed most of the weight much lower and at the center of the bike. They had a bunch of pockets too so I could stash stuff that I need to get at quickly – like my Bear Spray – I put it right next to my left leg so I could just reach down and grab it with my clutch hand. I also installed some hand guards. I bought them during the trip and paid twice what I would have back home. I was just about ready for a new rear tire as well, but it would have to wait until I got to Fairbanks since I couldn't find one in Whitehorse.

(Miles: 581)

PART 1 - (the day of the dog)

Ok. I had a bit more excitement today. I left Whitehorse early in the morning headed up the Klondike Highway bound for Dawson City. It was actually much earlier than I thought – it was rather challenging to keep track of time with the sun never really setting. It was also rather difficult to sleep as it never seemed to really get dark. But I was up and moving and the scenery was as incredible as ever.

A view of Five Finger Rapids on the Yukon River, from the Klondike Highway

I stopped for fuel at the first gas station on the Klondike Highway (Breaburn Lodge) at around 4:00 am. I didn't see anyone around so I tried the pump but it was turned off. I could see a few dogs lying around – they looked like a team of sled dogs. And one very friendly looking dog came over to me. I let him smell my hand and then patted him on the head. Nice dog! Then I started to walk over to the main building to see if anyone was there. As I got closer, three other "not so nice" dogs came charging at me, barking, growling and baring their teeth! They spread out and each came at me from a different direction. One got real close, so I put my hand out thinking he may calm down if I let him smell me – I think he was the leader. But he wasn't having any of that. He shot in and bit me on the leg - *Shit!* Luckily my motorcycle protective gear also worked pretty good against dog bites. But, I was backing up now and feeling a little nervous. They kept coming closer as I backed away so I kicked at one of them to get him to back off but they just kept inching closer. Then my animal instinct must have taken over because the fear quickly turned to anger.

"Alright Mr. Dog! You don't know who you're messin with. I've got written language, and opposing thumbs! I'm an ex-Army paratrooper, and former amateur boxer. AND, I watch the UFC "ALL" the time! - I'm gonna WHIP... YO... ASS!"

I got into a modified boxing stance and went after the closest one. He must have sensed that I meant business because he backed off instantly. Then I went after the next closest and he backed off too. After they had all retreated, I walked back to my bike to get my Bear Spray - I was going to teach these dogs a lesson. But then I thought it over and decided it probably wasn't a good idea. Not that I didn't want to – boy did I want to inflict a little pain on the dog that bit me. But I thought that there might be another animal with written language and opposing thumbs nearby who may own these dogs and have more firepower than pepper spray and a bowie knife. So, I left. But I was fuming for quite some time and even contemplated scheduling a return visit for my little friends. When I stopped at the next gas station, the lady there told me that there had been problems with the dogs there before and that someone was already suing the guy.

PART 2 - (the sleeping bag, the gas can, and the mosquitoes)

I arrived in Dawson City and was pleasantly surprised to find that it looked much like it must have nearly a hundred years earlier. The roads throughout the town were dirt, the sidewalks were made of wood, and the buildings looked like they were strait out of a wild-west cowboy movie.

The Downtown Hotel in Dawson City

It was a few days before the annual Dust to Dawson Run and the town was quiet. So, I talked to a few folks about the Dempster Highway and decided to ride it, and try to get back in time for the D2D Run festivities. My rear tire was questionable (nearly bald down the middle) but I figured I could probably make it if I took it easy. The Demptser Highway was unpaved, about 450 miles long, had lots of gravel and some pretty spectacular scenery as it crossed the Arctic Circle and traversed the Continental Divide. It went up to Inuvik in the Northwest Territories and it was the ONLY road that did - so it would be 900 miles of unpaved road up and back – *YESSS!!!* But, first I had to get a gas can - my bikes fuel range was 40 miles short of the distance between the first two fuel stops on the Dempster Highway. Then I repacked so I had enough room for the added gas can by leaving everything I didn't need for the Dempster ride behind. And the folks at the downtown hotel were nice enough to let me leave my extra gear there. I ended up leaving around 8:00pm and was just going to ride to a campground and stop for the night.

A view from North Fork Pass on the Dempster Highway

When I arrived at Engineer Creek Campground and began to set up my tent, I was attacked... again! This time by mosquitoes! At first there were only a few. No problem - I put on some insect repellent. But they seemed to arrive faster than they were being repelled. It was as if they called all their family, cousins, friends and neighbors, and said *"Hey come on over for some free food."* I found that if I moved to another spot, it would take them some time to find me but they always did. And the longer I stayed in one spot the more mosquitoes that would arrive. If I had stayed in one spot for a full minute, there would probably have been enough mosquitoes to pick me up and carry me away! It was time to flee! So, I threw everything back on the bike as fast as I could and took off. But in my haste, I did not secure everything as I should have. Down the road a little farther I felt the load shift behind me. My gas can was bumping me in the back so I stopped to check it, and discovered that my duffle bag, with my sleeping bag and extra clothes, was gone. It had been strapped on to the back rack with a bungee cord and when I found it on the road a ways back, it was fried! It must have dangled over the exhaust for a while which disintegrated the sleeping bag along with almost everything else in the duffle bag - both the duffle and sleeping bags were made of synthetic materials. I wonder if I looked anything like the Ghost Rider as I was flying along the Dempster Highway with flames dancing off the back of my bike. Guess I'm lucky that it didn't catch the GAS CAN on fire!

My toasted sleeping bag

Early morning on the Dempster Highway a few days before summer solstice

Anyway, I couldn't camp out after that so I forged on. But when I got to Eagle Plains they were closed. Eagle Plains is about halfway up the Dempster and consists of a gas station, hotel, and restaurant all in one. So, I had to wait until morning to get fuel. Unfortunately, no one was awake at the hotel. But they did leave the front door unlocked, so I slept in the lobby.

(Miles: 225)

I woke up early - I had no choice, I was sleeping in the lobby. After eating breakfast in the small cafeteria, I fueled up and headed out. The Dempster Highway crossed the Peel and Mackenzie Rivers with the use of ferries. The ferry landings were deep gravel and required careful negotiation on a motorcycle. The first ferry operator warned me about this. So I was cautious and managed to load and disembark both ferries without incident.

Waiting for the ferry

Peel River Ferry Crossing

Getting ready to go

After crossing the second river I arrived in Inuvik, on the Mackenzie Delta, in the Northwest Territories of Canada. Inuvik is the most northerly town to which one can drive, without waiting for winter to freeze the rivers. After having some lunch at a café in town I went looking for gas and met Larry at the station, washing his bike. He and another rider, Miles, had ridden up from Alberta Canada on a couple KTM's. After talking for a bit, I followed Larry to the Arctic Chalet cabins where they were staying and got a room. He and Miles were headed back down the Dempster in the morning so I would have some riding companions for the trip south. Except for a few hours one afternoon, I had been riding solo since left my home in Southern California – so I surely welcomed a little company.

Miles and Larry on the Dempster near Ft. McPherson

Day 11 – Inuvik, Northwest Territories to Dawson City to Dempster Corner, Yukon

(Miles: 500)

I rode all the way down the Dempster Highway with Larry and Miles – it was great fun! But I was still getting use to riding in gravel - these guys grew up riding in the stuff. Nevertheless, I'd ridden a lot in the dirt so I was doing alright.

We stopped in Fort McPherson for gas and the gal working at the station told us they were having a barbeque to celebrate Aboriginal Day and invited us to join them, so we did. They cooked up some burgers, hot dogs, and fresh white fish. The whole town was there - what a treat to be invited to join them for the celebration. And, we weren't the only ones they invited. Everyone that stopped for gas ended up at the barbeque. Really nice people!

Celebration at Fort McPherson

The barbeque

They even had live music

One of the town elders told us about some of the village's history. In 1932 the notorious, Mad Trapper of Rat River holed up there before he was eventually caught and killed in a shootout after a 150 mile chase on foot. The whole thing turned into a media circus as he eluded the Royal Canadian Mounted Police (RCMP) for over a month. But, the settlement was most famous for the "Lost Patrol." During the early 1900's the RCMP carried mail, once each year, the 460 miles from Dawson City to Fort McPherson. A four man patrol with 3 dog teams and 30 days of supplies left Fort McPherson in December of 1910 and basically got lost - they never made it back to Dawson City - all 4 men died in route.

One of the village elders and the local historian

This tiny cabin belonged to the Mad Trapper of Rat River

**Larry, Miles and the village historian in the town cemetery
around the flag pole on the grave site for the Lost Patrol**

We also visited the Fort McPherson Tent & Canvas
Company while we were in town. They make all sorts of
stuff out of canvas, mainly tents, packs, and such. I wanted
to get something small as a souvenir so I bought a map
case. But, it didn't have their really cool tag with their logo
on it that says "Made in Canada's Arctic." So, they gave me
one and I had it stitched on later – they would have sewn it
on for me but everyone was at the barbeque.

After that we took off - and the rest of the ride down
the Dempster was loads of fun. Riding along thru such a
beautiful area on such a fun road for such a long distance
was absolutely incredible. I remember thinking *"Wow – I
wonder if this is what it would be like to race in the Baja
1000. Hmmm... maybe I could do that next!"* At that
point it should have been obvious that I had become an
Adventure Junkie – there I was in the middle of an
incredibly colossal journey, and thinking about taking on

yet another mammoth Adventure. But I was having the time of my life in my current escapade – a pleasantly entertaining, groomed, gravel road through the rugged wilderness of the Yukon and Northwest Territories of Canada that seemed to stretch out forever in front of us. I distinctly remember thinking as I flew along that narrow strip of dirt and rock - at one with the road - *Ah... life is good!*

200 miles down, 250 miles to go!

Posing at the Circle

Taking a break on the North Fork Pass

Miles making some roadside adjustments

Larry repacking his gear

When we reached the bottom of the Dempster Highway, we went into Dawson City to get a room but there were none available because everyone had arrived for the Dust to Dawson Run. Main Street was lined with Dual-Sport and Adventure style motorcycles and the town was teeming with riders.

Main Street in Dawson City during the D2D Run

Lots of big BMW Adventure bikes

Larry at the D2D - this guy was the real deal.

So, we went back to the Dempster Junction and got an overflow room at the hotel there. It was actually more of a bunkhouse with two sets of bunk beds - the showers and restrooms were shared. It was a real bargain though, especially split 3 ways. And the host there told us the overflow rooms were available even when the hotel was not full. It was perfect for Adventure touring on a budget.

(Miles: 100)

We all went into Dawson City in the morning and met some of the other folks that had come in for the D2D Run. There were lots of people hanging out around the bikes and talking about riding. I talked to the owner of the Downtown Hotel and he told me he had a new rear tire that would fit my bike – and he said the guys at the auto parts could install it for me. So off I went, new tire in hand.

I got back to the festivities just in time for the Poker run and it was an absolute blast! They handed out route maps that took us to 5 checkpoints around a 60 mile loop. It started out rather mellow but quickly escalated into an all-out race from one check point to the next. While there were many who maintained their composure throughout, some were blasting thru the terrain as fast as they could go. But, the maps were not exactly spot on - or perhaps it was our navigation that wasn't exactly right. Anyway, the fastest were not always first to arrive. Checkpoint number one was at the top of a hill and everyone pretty much found it at the same time. The sight of all these bikes (all types - competition bikes to casual dual sports, singles, big twins, even a couple cruisers) blasting up this hill, 3 and 4 wide - it was hysterical. And it only escalated from there. I for one was a bit on the overanxious side. I recall flying passed a couple big Adventure bikes while racing with Miles down a nicely groomed dirt road power-sliding thru a turn as we raced toward the next checkpoint. Fortunately, there were no incidents and everyone had a great time. But later during a speech at the official D2D dinner, our rowdy hooligan riding was gently admonished. While we weren't the only ones riding fast, we were probably riding faster than anyone else and undoubtedly justified the candid lecture. But there were no hard feelings and in the end it was all good!

There were also some fun bike games for all to participate in. Unfortunately I missed most of the games but between us we did get a few pictures.

Let the game begin.

Miles during one of the games

After the festivities ended we headed back to Demptser Corner where we were staying. And, on the way back a huge moose (or swamp donkey) walked out onto the road right in front of Miles. I thought for sure he was going to hit it! He said that he could have reached out and touched it as he went by. I was following him – but I stomped on the brakes and skidded to a stop. Then the moose just sauntered off.

Day 13 - Dawson City, Yukon to Forty Mile to Tok, Alaska

(Miles: 230)

We ate breakfast at the Dempster Corner café. While we were eating, we talked with a young lady whose car was stuck up on the Dempster Highway with a couple flat tires. Someone had taken her wheels in to Dawson City the night before but the service station was closed. We felt like we should do something to help but weren't sure what so we said good luck and goodbye.

We all needed oil changes so we went back to Dawson City, to the Auto Parts store. We purchased our oil there and they were nice enough to let us change it in back by their shop. We were all feeling like we should have helped the woman back at Dempster Corner so we decided to see about picking up her wheels, purchasing some tires, and sending them out to her but someone had beat us to it and already picked up the wheels.

So we set out for Alaska over the "Top of the World" highway but made a slight detour to check out Forty Mile - one of the first settlements in the Yukon. Our detour took us about 20 miles up the Taylor highway – another scenic dirt road, and then we hiked about another mile to Fortymile. Two Aboriginals (Vic and Jack) were there doing some maintenance of the grounds and after we finished looking around and talking they gave us a ride in their boat, on the Yukon River, back to our bikes. Nice people!

Larry and Jack

Me, Vic, and Miles

Then off we went, to Alaska. Just before the border, on the right, there was a hilltop summit. There was no trail and I had to dodge some larger rocks but I was actually able to ride up it on my trusty DR. At the top was an "Inukshuk" (a stack of rocks that formed a sort of landmark) - one of the rocks was placed there by me. The view was well worth the climb – it was absolutely incredible! Looking down over a sea of descending mountains, in all directions - for as far as the eye could see. It actually felt like I was on top of the world! But it also felt kind of strange - almost like I shouldn't be there. I even forgot to take a picture.

Then I rode down and went across the border, we took the obligatory, "Welcome to Alaska" sign, pictures and went on to Chicken and then Tok where we found some other folks from the D2D Run and stayed for the night.

Larry and Miles at the Alaska sign on the Top of the World Highway

Yours truly fighting off a Grizzly in a Tok restaurant

Day 14 - Tok to Fairbanks via the Tok Cutoff and the Denali Highway

(Miles: 461)

Miles opted to start heading back toward home. And, Larry and I headed for Fairbanks via the long, bumpy, scenic route – the Tok Cutoff and the Denali Highway. We had been talking to a guy riding a sport bike the night before and he said the Tok Cutoff was scenic but the road was terrible - which sounded like a great ride to us. The road had a lot of frost heaves that made it a blast on dual-sport bikes with lots of suspension - kind of like a rollercoaster or a bunch of giant whoop-de-doos.

Then we got to the Denali Highway and I can't even begin to tell you how much fun this road was! It's mostly dirt with just a bit of gravel and it was smooth and twisty so you could really have fun on it. I was having a blast, pitching it sideways and power-sliding around turns, pinning it down the straits - probably not being a model citizen but having a great time in the dirt! Although I did lose my gas can to another bungee cord failure. It seemed that whenever I started having too much fun in the dirt, stuff would start falling off my bike. Anyway, the scenery was so unbelievable that you wanted to slow down and see it too. And therein lays the dilemma: speed up and have fun on this great dirt road, or slow down and enjoy the scenery - maybe even stop to take pictures. Well I only took a few pictures - but man did I have fun! Absolutely unbelievable!

Wow what an incredible view - slow down; Wow, what a fun road - speed up.

It was just like that, back and forth the whole way - all 130 miles of it. Did I say I only took a few pictures? I don't know what happened but I couldn't find any of them. Oh well! What a fun road!

Day 15 - Fairbanks to Kenny Lake

(Miles: 286)

When we got to Fairbanks Larry's fork seals were leaking and my bike had developed an oil leak (a faulty base gasket design on the earlier DR650's). Unfortunately, the Suzuki dealer was closed on Mondays. So, off we went to the KTM dealer - a real nice guy with a shop right behind his house, just outside of Fairbanks. Larry got his fork seals taken care of. I got a kayak bag for my clothes in town – I was slowly becoming a seasoned adventure rider.

Our next destination was McCarthy, or actually the road that led to McCarthy - it's all about the ride. Anyway, we stopped at Kenny Lake and stayed in a rustic cabin with electricity and a couple sets of bunk beds - the shared shower/restroom was in the main building.

Heading south on the Richardson Highway

Another beautiful view along the Richardson Highway

On the Richardson near the beginning of the Denali Highway

(Miles: 260)

We were off to tackle another great road - McCarthy Road... and more beautiful scenery - it just didn't stop. The road was about two thirds gravel and went out to the town of McCarthy and the old Kennecott Copper Mines. It was a fun easy ride out to McCarthy even with lots of stops for pictures along the way. After a quick tour of the site we turned around and headed for Valdez.

We arrived in Valdez fairly early and bought tickets on the ferry which would take us across the Prince William Sound to Whittier the next morning. From there we could ride to Anchorage.

Along the first part of McCarthy Road

Narrow bridge at beginning of gravel section of McCarthy Road

Atop the narrow bridge

Farther along McCarthy Road

View from McCarthy Road

Kennecott Mill

A quick tour of the Mill

Onward to Valdez

Worthington Glacier

Chugach Mountains above Valdez

Valdez Marina

(Miles: 60 + 5 hour ferry ride)

We got on the ferry early and I took a long nap on the upper deck. They had lounge chairs and many of the folks aboard had sleeping bags – but I still hadn't replaced mine. The ride was scenic and we got to see a few glaciers from a distance.

Napping on the Ferry Ride

Glaciers along Prince William Sound

After the ferry arrived in Whittier we had to ride thru the 2.6 mile long, Anton Anderson Memorial tunnel on the way to Anchorage. The tunnel was shared by trains and road vehicles, and access would alternate between the two. So there were railroad tracks running the length of the tunnel as well. And, they made the motorcycles go last just in case someone fell in the tunnel – which could easily happen because motorcycles had to ride between the train tracks.

When we got to Anchorage we stopped at a motorcycle shop called: "The Motorcycle Shop" to get another rear tire for Larry. While we were there I found some "real" soft side-bags and a new jacket. After that we stopped at Alaska Leather and Larry bought a new helmet because his old one fell apart. We should have gotten the tire there too as Barb, the owner, had a much better selection.

We met Barb at the D2D Run and later we heard that she had crash on her way home from Dawson City. We heard the news from a number of people we had run into after leaving Dawson City. Apparently, she did a big ole tank slapper before going down, and motorcycle news traveled surprisingly fast in Alaska. If you crashed, you were immediately famous! Back in Dawson City we had heard about a guy on a Triumph who crashed on the Dempster Highway and later I met him at the Suzuki dealer in Fairbanks. He pulled in on a banged up Triumph Tiger and I knew it was him. *Hey! I heard about you! He grins - yeah, that was me.*

(Miles: 865)

Ok. We decided to ride the Dalton Highway or the Haul Road as it is often referred. Actually, Larry decided to; I had planned to all along. But, he was on a little tighter schedule so he didn't know if he would have enough time.

If you are not familiar with the area in question, allow me to enlighten you. The Dalton Highway is about 415 miles long, mostly gravel and dirt with some pavement. It goes to the town of Deadhorse - as far north as you can go on a road in Alaska. Many people tackle the Dalton in 4 days - two up; two back. The more hard core will do it in 2 days - one up; one back. And, most people start from Fairbanks which is about 80 miles south of the Dalton Highway. Anchorage is about 450 miles south of the Dalton.

So, we left Anchorage at about 8:00am and rode strait thru to Fairbanks except for a short stop at Denali National Park to take in a quick view of Mt. McKinley and get a bite to eat. It was an easy ride on pavement and once again the scenery was beautiful.

Mt. McKinley, aka Denali

We arrived in Fairbanks around 4:00pm and dropped off everything that we didn't need at the KTM dealer. I even removed my windscreen for the ride up the Dalton - I never put it on back either and I never even missed it!

Windscreen? We don't need no stinking windscreen – we're adventure riders!

Then we headed for the Dalton. When we reached the start of the famous Haul Road we had already travelled 450 miles on pavement - it was late afternoon and we were just getting started.

Larry and I near the start of the Dalton.

There was a construction zone just before the beginning of the Dalton and the road was pretty torn up – it was just starting to get fun. A few hours later we reached our first gas stop at the Yukon River Camp and had a bite to eat. We talked with a guy on a big BMW who was on his way back down. Basically he told us the same thing that everyone else told us – *"watch the pea gravel on the last 50 miles - just go slow!"* And, he said the temperature dropped drastically near the end. *OK. No big deal.* So off we went.

Crossing the Arctic Circle... again

we rode another 120 miles to the next gas stop in Coldfoot – by then it was getting late and a little chilly. We had some soup to warm up a bit and when we were leaving the guy behind the counter told us that there would probably be fog by the time we descended toward Deadhorse. *I'm thinking FOG! - what's a little fog gonna matter!* So, we fueled up again (we filled the gas can too –

we would need it to reach Deadhorse) and off we went. Of course, the scenery was awesome - as usual.

The Brooks Range Pass

About 100 miles further and temperature had dropped quite a bit. When we started to descend, about 80 miles from Deadhorse, we could see the fog and it was getting colder. I was wearing leather sports-bike gloves and my fingers were freezing. Knowing that we still had a ways to go, I began stopping to thaw my fingers whenever I couldn't feel them anymore. Larry, the experienced adventure rider he was, had warm gloves and heated grips.

We started running into the pea gravel about 50 miles from Deadhorse as advertised. So I started going slower and stopping more often to thaw my hands. By then my visor was fogging on the inside and getting covered by the mist from the fog on the outside - so, I had to leave it open to see. The pea gravel was getting deeper too. And, it was getting colder! Larry had gone ahead but stopped to see if I was alright. When I told him I was stopping to thaw my hands, he gave me his warm gloves and turned his heated grips up to high. I told him I couldn't see either - and he said: "go 110 (kph) and it will blow the mist off your visor." *A Hundred and Ten! What about the pea gravel?* It's no big deal he says - I'll see you there. By then we were about 25 miles from Deadhorse and the wind was starting to blow. So, I closed my visor and took off.

I got up to about 100 and I couldn't see shit! So, I opened my visor to see - but then I had to squint and continuously blink because the freezing fog felt like pins sticking me in the eyes. After about 10 miles of that, I started to think that maybe I had bitten off more than I could chew. I was flying thru the pea gravel (everyone said to go slow), my face was frozen, I could barely see, the wind was starting to blow harder and the ice fog was getting thicker - *it's a Freaking Blizzard! I start thinking, what if I crash or get a flat? OK. This is no longer just an entertaining adventure. The dangers of motorcycling in the Arctic are becoming a harsh reality for me.*

Now I'm getting cold all over. How much farther? Will I make it? I can't see shit! I ride another ten miles. I'm not stopping for anything now. The wind is blowing even harder - I have to lean the bike into the wind just to stay upright. I'm riding with my eyes virtually closed - opening them just often enough to determine my general direction. I've almost reached the point of apathy when I see the first building. A few more miles and I reach the main town. I find the Prudhoe Bay hotel and Larry is there. "It looks like a storm's coming in, and we could get stuck here for a few days" he says. Oh well. I was just glad to be indoors. Then Larry says: "I'm going back." *GOING BACK? NOW? I wouldn't go back now if the sun was shining and it was a nice warm day! There's a blizzard out there! And, I'm exhausted. I'm not going anywhere! If I get stuck here for 3 days - oh well.* Then Larry says: "I can't afford to get stuck here for 3 days." He's a Rancher - and one tough dude! Larry figured that he could ride back out of the storm just like we had ridden into it. So, we had a cup of coffee in the cafeteria and off he went. I got a room and went to sleep. What a day!

Descending toward Prudhoe Bay and the Arctic Ocean

Just before it really started getting cold

(Miles 496)

Well I slept for about 6 hours then got up and had breakfast in the cafeteria. All meals were included in the cost of the room at the Prudhoe Bay Hotel. It was a real bargain. The Hotel itself was nothing fancy - far from it. It looked like a giant construction trailer. But, it was kind of cool because that's where all the oil workers stayed. So, you got an idea of what life was like up there. I was surprised by the number of women that were working there. I guess the pay was pretty good but they stayed there for a month at a time. Anyway, I had breakfast with an electrician who was just up there for the next couple days.

After breakfast I went outside to check on my bike. There was another rider getting ready to leave. He had ridden up two days ago and took a full day to recuperate before heading back. When I told him that I'd ridden up from Anchorage the night before, he said: WOW! You are THE MAN! Nope, I said. The guy I rode up here with turned right around and rode back to Fairbanks - HE's THE MAN!

Later I went to see about the Prudhoe Bay tour. If you wanted to go the last couple miles to the Arctic Ocean you had to go on a tour because it was on private property. But, I found out that you needed to schedule the tour 24 hours in advance so I ditched that idea and started thinking about heading back.

First I needed another gas can - I lost mine on the Denali Highway and hadn't replaced it. I used Larry's can on the way up there but he was gone and he took his gas can with him. I asked around and was told that they would have one at the Deadhorse General Store. I also needed some warm gloves and a couple bungee cords. A nice guy named Dave helped me locate everything and rang it up. I was thinking "they're really going to stick it to me here because we're way out in the middle of nowhere." But, to my surprise, the total was $20. Wow, that was cheap! The gloves alone would probably have cost that much back home (I got some really warm gloves). So, if you go to Prudhoe Bay/Deadhorse and need something while you're there, don't hesitate to swing by the General Store.

The Prudhoe Bay Sign - just before heading back.

Next I headed over to fuel up the bike and the gas can. Then I was set to head back down the Dalton and away I went. It is much warmer than it was a day earlier so I didn't really even need the warm gloves. It was a beautiful day to be riding the Dalton.

At one point I recall riding along thinking about how I was on this big adventure and patting myself on the back when I came across a guy on a bicycle! YUP! *Are you kidding! Guess I'm not really that adventurous after all!* But I was moving at a pretty good pace on my way down the Dalton. I know it's not a race but I was riding way faster than that guy - sure he was riding a bicycle... thru gravel, but I'm just saying! LOL Seriously though, my hat is off to those adventurous souls travelling the far reaches of the globe on bicycles.

Anyhow, after dumping the gas can into my tank I reached Coldfoot and stopped to refuel. I thought about refilling the can but decided that I wouldn't need it. *DOH!*

Truck on the Dalton

So, off I went again. My speed was averaging 75-80mph and occasionally even higher – and I was having a blast.

Suddenly the rear wheel locks up and I begin to fishtail wildly. I pull in the clutch but the wheel is still locked up. So, I just steer my fishtailing bike as straight as I can, for what feels like an eternity, until it finally comes to a stop. WOW! That was pretty exciting!

I hopped off the bike to see what the problem was and found that my kayak bag had fallen off the rack, dangled over the side, and wedged between the rear tire and the swing arm. Another bungee cord failure – *Ok!* I pulled it out, strapped it back on the rack and away I went.

A while later I arrived at the Yukon River Camp, my last gas stop on the Dalton Highway. When I got there, they were closed. And there was a sign on the gas pump that said: "Out of Unleaded." *Shoot! Now what?* I didn't fill the gas can at the last stop and I only had enough gas to go about 60 miles – it was about 90 miles to the next gas. Ok, I thought that if I took it slow, maybe I could make it. So I rode 40 mph for the next hour and checked my fuel level. It was pretty low and I still had 50 miles to go.

I started riding up the hills, then shutting off the engine and coasting down the hills. It was about 2:00am and kind of eerie when I was coasting along on the downhill's with the motor off. I noticed a thumping sound and realized it must be a flat spot on my tire from when it locked up the rear wheel - later I took a look and I'm lucky it didn't go flat as it was worn pretty thin at that spot. I finally made it to the next gas and after refueling, I was off at full speed again.

When I arrived in Fairbanks it was about 3:00am. So, I went back to the same hotel where Larry and I had stayed before and got a room. Then when I went to move my bike to the parking lot, I saw a KTM just like Larry's - *hmmm, it is Larry's!*

(Miles: 204)

I had left a message for Larry at the front desk and he called my room in the morning. We both needed maintenance on our bikes so after breakfast he went over to the KTM dealer and I went to the Suzuki shop. I got 2 new tires and an oil change then headed over to the KTM dealer. Larry did an oil change, got a new rear tire, and adjusted his valves. By then it was late afternoon but we headed out anyway.

I saw another bicycle rider that day. But, this guy was carrying camping and fishing gear – he was dressed in a very leisurely fashion wearing a fishing hat and looked like he was in no particular hurry to get anywhere. I slowly rotated my head, taking a good long look at his bike and gear as I rode passed - several fishing poles were strapped to the back - and I recall thinking to myself: *that guy has it all figured out!*

But our trips were coming to an end and it was time to start heading for home. After few hours it started to rain pretty hard. I was grateful that it hadn't rained much at the beginning of my trip or it would not have been nearly as enjoyable. We considered ourselves fortunate as summertime is the rainy season in Alaska. But, it looked like our luck had run out as the sky's darkened and the rain fell. So, we decided to call it a day when we reached Tok.

(*Miles* 496)

The day started out clear, but the weather report looked bleak and it rained for the last 6 hours. Fortunately it was mostly pavement that day and we still made some decent mileage before stopping for the night in Teslin.

Our route along the Alcan that day took us through Whitehorse. I didn't know it at the time but Makiko Sugino, a Japanese woman who had been on the road for nearly 5 years on a trip around the world, had stopped in Whitehorse – she was there that very day we rode through. I'd read that she was hard to miss as she was riding a 250 and rarely went faster than about 45 mph. Several people on ADVRIDER had posted information about her incredible journey and a quick internet search revealed that others had crossed paths with her in the far corners of the earth. I certainly would have stopped and tried to find and meet her if I had only known she was there. I've had a number of near misses like that throughout my life.

Oh well... not quite,

two ships crossing in the night.

Just before it started raining

Kluane Lake

A Construction Zone on the Alcan

(Miles 753)

Larry and I went our separate ways as he headed east to Alberta and I went south to ride the Cassiar Highway – yet another great road. It started out a narrow dirt road with twisties, scenery and wildlife and just got better from there. I saw a brown bear near the beginning just walking on the side of the road - that got my heart beating a little faster. It was still raining on and off but around noon I rode out of the storm and into the sunshine. Unfortunately for Larry, the storm was moving east with him.

A couple hours later I stopped at a rest area and met a guy from England riding a Motoguzzi and travelling the opposite direction. I told him that it was raining where he was going and he told me that he had seen 5 bears where I was going. Sure enough, I saw 4 more bears myself - each time they just ran off when they heard me coming. I don't usually agree with the old Harley riders moto "Loud pipes save lives" but I think it may actually have some merit up there.

I wanted to try for a 1,000 mile day somewhere along the trip home and today looked like a possible candidate. But it didn't happen as it started raining again later in the evening.

Somewhere along the Northern Cassiar

The Cassiar - after leaving the rain behind

Kluachon

Southern Cassiar

Bell II

Missed the turn off and ended up here at Bear Glacier - 100
miles out of my way but the view was nice.

Day 23 - Burns Lake, British Columbia, Canada to Bellingham, Washington, USA

(Miles 609)

I made another attempt at doing 1,000 miles in a single day but again, it didn't happen. I did however manage to get a speeding ticket. I had begun my return to a world I was more familiar with. I was leaving the sparsely populated rural regions of the north for the warmer, more densely populated areas to the south. I could see it in the scenery and I could see it in the people – gradual subtle changes in both but still evident.

I crossed the border into the U.S. in the small town of Sumas, to much less fanfare than my previous experience going into Vancouver British Colombia on my way north. But I was back on American soil, in the lower 48 – and as I travelled south, the days were getting warmer and shorter.

(Miles 270)

I stopped just south of Seattle to get another rear tire. I knew the one I had wouldn't make it home and I wanted one more try at a 1,000 mile day. The shop I stopped at had a nice collection of vintage bikes including a nicely restored example of the first motorcycle I ever owned – a 1965 Honda 50 Super Cub.

Looking at that bike brought back memories of my childhood. I learned to ride on that bike. And I started learning about mechanics – through necessity. I bent the pushrods once by revving the motor too high and I was able to fix it by laying them on a flat surface and hammering them strait again... life was much simpler back then.

It was also the 4th of July so, I called my sister who lived nearby and was able to celebrate the holiday with her family and friends. It was nice to share a little time with my sister but I still had some distance to cover before my vacation ended so I was back on the road in the morning.

(Miles 1,067)

This was the last chance I would have at doing 1,000 miles in a single day. I planned to take Interstate 5, the multilane super-slab, for about 120 miles and the rest was two-lane, secondary roads. Not the easiest way to go 1,000 miles on a motorcycle - secondary roads on a thumper - what was I thinking? Anyway, the ride was scenic and fun - at least the first seven-hundred miles! The last 300 miles seemed to take for-ever! And, I almost didn't make it.

Somewhere around Bishop California, just a few hundred miles from home, I spotted a deer standing on the right shoulder of the road, only seconds before he bolted out in front of me. I missed him by about a foot as he dashed between me and an oncoming car. *That was close!* I stopped to clean the bugs off my face shield and check my shorts.

It also got up over 100 degrees passing thru parts of Northern California earlier in the day. And, when I went by Death Valley, it was unbelievably hot, especially considering that it was around midnight – a rather shocking contrast to what I had experienced up in the Arctic only a week earlier.

A few hours later I stopped again – I was travelling a very desolate stretch of desert road just a few hours north of home. But I was very tired so I just stopped right in the middle of the dark, deserted two-lane road. It was nearly pitch black and eerily quiet.

My incredible journey was coming to an end and it would soon become obvious as I rode the last hundred miles from the isolation of the lonely desert into the enormous concrete jungle known as the greater Los Angeles area – as the miles ticked by that two-lane road grew into a 12-lane superhighway. I finally rolled into my driveway, safe and sound, a mere 21 hours and 1,067 miles after leaving my sister's house the previous morning. I did it!

My adventure was over. Many great roads, many wonderful people, and more than a few thrilling moments - 11,260 miles, 25 days, 5 bears, 4 tires, 3 close encounters, 2 oil changes, 2x out of gas, 1 crash, 1 fire, 1 blizzard, 1 dog fight, 1 thousand mile day, and 1 conversation with God!

Ironically, this was supposed to be my last great adventure. But when I returned home, I realized that my plantar fasciitis was gone! I had lost nearly 20 pounds and I felt 20 years younger. So as it turned out, this was just the beginning.

Thank you for letting me share my experience with you.

www.airborneandy.com

The End

CPSIA information can be obtained
at www.ICGtesting.com
Printed in the USA
LVHW111647140222
711060LV00026B/573

9 781482 367317